SACKCLOTH & ASHES

For the Lord himself shall descend from heaven with a shout, with the voice of the archangel, and with the trump of God: and **the dead in Christ shall rise first:**
<u>1 Thessalonians 4:16 KJV</u>

GLORIA A. PERALES

Copyright © 2022 Gloria A. Perales.
All rights reserved.

ISBN: 979-8-88640-520-0 (sc)
ISBN: 979-8-88640-521-7 (hc)
ISBN: 979-8-88640-522-4 (e)

Because of the dynamic nature of the Internet, any web addresses or links contained in this book may have changed since publication and may no longer be valid. The views expressed in this work are solely those of the author and do not necessarily reflect the views of the publisher, and the publisher hereby disclaims any responsibility for them.

One Galleria Blvd., Suite 1900, Metairie, LA 70001
1-888-421-2397

CONTENTS

Introduction 1
Who are We? 3
What is Unconditional Love? 4
What is Unconditional Repentence? 6
Draw Near to the Lord… 10
My Prayers Will be Answered 11
Unconditional Mercy! 13
Sackcloth & Ashes 15
What is the Sign of Jonah? 15
The Sign of Jonah 15
What is Sackcloth And Ashes? 18
How to Use Sackcloth & What to Do! 18
What You Must Do Once You Have it on or are
    Laying or Sitting On it 22
Pray With Your Own Words 24
Suggested Scriptures To Read 25
In the Old Testament 25
Sins to Confess While Using Sackcloth & Ashes 28
Additonal Sins - Woes in the Book of Matthew 36
Why Did Mary Present the Scapular as a
    Sign of Salvation? 40
Todays Message is This 43
Believe! 46
References 49

INTRODUCTION

This book includes scriptures from the New Testament and the Old Testament that refer to sackcloth and ashes. They open our eyes and hearts to the possibility of regaining our health and being relieved of our burdens.

In the New Testament it clearly states that if Tyre and Sidon would have done what we have done, **"they would have repented long ago, sitting in sackcloth and ashes."** We are being told to sit in sackcloth and ashes and that we should be aware of what we have done. In the book of Revelations, the two witnesses wear sackcloth for three and a half years.

> *Woe unto thee, Chorazin! Woe unto thee, Bethsaida! for if the mighty works had been done in Tyre and Sidon, which were done in you,* ***they would have repented long ago, sitting in sackcloth and ashes****.*
> <u>Matthew 11:21 NKJV</u>

> *And I will give unto my two witnesses, and they shall prophesy a thousand two hundred and threescore days, clothed in sackcloth.*
> <u>Revelation 11:3 KJV</u>

I also explain how the Lord taught me to use sackcloth and ashes. I felt weird especially in this generation. I was amazed that after I had first completed repenting in Sackcloth with use of ashes and opened my bible, the Lord fixed my eyes on the following scripture:

> *You have turned for me my mourning into dancing;*
> *You have loosed my sackcloth and girded me with gladness,*
> <u>Psalm 30:11 NASB95</u>

I probably started using sackcloth in 2004 and then began sleeping in it. I stopped after my mother passed away in 2011, not sure exactly when. Anyway, the morning of March 26, 2007 after a series of events that occurred that weekend, I woke up and received a distinct thought not my own. It said to me:

> **"a multitude of your sins are forgiven you for you have loved much".**

My response to that thought was:

"Thank you, Lord!

A M U L T I T U D E ?

I had that many?

What about the rest of them?

How do I get rid of those?" Oh my God!!!

And so the struggle continues… running the race as the apostles mentioned in the bible. Sadly, I am still a sinner…

WHO ARE WE?

Paul refers to us as being earthen vessels.

> [7]*But we have this treasure*
> *in earthen vessels,*
> *that the excellency of the power*
> *may be of God, and not of us.*
> *2 Cor 4:7 KJV*

I can only wonder what has been hidden from us. If the excellency of the power of God, who is perfect, is not in us, then what is? The power of us? The power of the evil one? I would hope not! But …

> [19]*We know that we are of God,*
> *and that the whole world lies*
> in the power of the evil one.
> *1 John 5:19 NASB*

We must strive to empty ourselves of our wicked ways. How many of our ancestors' sins do we hold in these earthen vessels of ours? and what are they?

Jesus taught unconditional love, unconditional forgiveness, and unconditional mercy. John the Baptist spoke repentance and the Apostles continued to speak repentance, love, and mercy even after the crucifixion. And so, it is imperative that we do as Jesus has taught. He is the Way! And as scripture tells us in *Matthew 11:21* we should have repented long ago in sackcloth and ashes.

WHAT IS UNCONDITIONAL LOVE?

ABOUT US... THE LIVING
NEW ERA of UNCONDITIONAL LOVE

Master, which is the great commandment in the law?
Jesus said unto him,
Thou shalt love the Lord thy God
with all thy heart, and with all thy soul,
and with all thy mind.
This is the first and great commandment.
And the second is like unto it,
Thou shalt love thy neighbour as thyself.
On these two commandments ***hang all the law***
and the prophets. Mathew 22:36-40 KJV

The Lord mentioned that upon the great commandments "hangs all the law" and the prophets. In other words, demonstrating and living in unconditional love automatically results in unconditional mercy, unconditional forgiveness towards everyone and obedience to His commands.

Jesus came to convert us, and make believers out of us. We who are for Him believe that God became man in Jesus Christ. His Omnipotent Love and Excruciating Passion of dying on the cross, is one no man can perceive or could have endured without the grace Our Heavenly Father bestowed upon Jesus. His passion was truly beyond our understanding and the Love demonstrated beyond our comprehension.

We must surrender to Him and reciprocate! That is, follow His examples, do as he did. Love unconditionally as He loves! Forgive the worst of sinners! Forgive those who have hurt us the most! Forgive no matter what the stumbling block may be or may have been!

> *By this we know love,*
> *because He laid down His life for us.*
> *And we also ought to lay down our lives*
> *for the brethren*
> <u>*1 John 3:16 NKJV*</u>

ABOUT THEM… THE LIVING DEAD
The Dead Who Are Living in Spirit

Since Adam and Eve, there are so many souls who have passed and may be suffering during their purification in purgatory or wherever they may be. Perhaps we are their only hope, repenting for them, asking for forgiveness for them, being merciful to them and loving them too.

The following scripture says that the dead in Christ will rise first. Why has it taken so long? Perhaps because of our neglect.

> *For the Lord himself shall descend from heaven*
> *with a shout, with the voice of the archangel,*
> *and with the trump of God: and*
> **the dead in Christ shall rise first:**
> <u>*1 Thessalonians 4:16 KJV*</u>

I am believing that repenting without conditions, "unconditional repentance" will help not only us, but also those who are the living dead (alive in spirit), even the worst of sinners. Maybe Judas, whose actions were for the glory of Our Lord is still suffering. Or Ramsey the Pharaoh, whom the Lord used to demonstrate His great works. I do hope all the deceased will benefit from our prayers and our repentance for them.

I believe that our repentance for them will help them **to be <u>with</u> the dead first to rise** as noted in *1Thess 4:16*.

We must pray for them. **The Lord wants everyone to be saved.** Surely, our ancestors have sins from prior generations and on it goes...

WHAT IS UNCONDITIONAL REPENTENCE?

I thought I was born again as preachers have taught in churches such as non-denominational, Pentecostal and others alike.

However, now knowing, that I was informed that I had a multitude of sins that I did not know existed, I was alarmed. Consequently, I began looking for sins to confess. I looked for sins that were listed in the bible or anywhere and included them in this book. I was seeking unconditional repentance hoping to be relieved of them. I am sure there are many I have omitted out of ignorance. If you think of additional sins please confess them for me, and for the whole world living and the dead.

We all make the same sins. We are all sinners. Jesus came to preach love and repentance and so, I believe this is our solution, to do as He does or has asked us to do. It is important to repent in sackcloth and use ashes.

Are we all required to use it? Are we required to wear it? Pray about it, ask the Lord. If you sincerely repent, I have no doubt that in His time, He will answer!

Perhaps the answer is in the following scripture and the glory of the Lord will be our reward:

> *Isaiah 58:6-8 KJV*
> *⁶Is not this the fast that I have chosen?*
> **to loose the bands of wickedness,**
> **to undo the heavy burdens,**
> **and to let the oppressed go free,**
> **and that ye break every yoke?**
> *⁷Is it not to* **deal thy bread to the hungry**,
> *and that thou* **bring the poor that are cast out**
> **to thy house?**
> *when thou seest* **the naked, that thou cover him**;
> *and that thou hide not thyself from thine own flesh?*
> *⁸**Then shall thy light break forth** as the morning,*
> and **thine health shall spring forth speedily:**
> **and thy righteousness shall go before thee;**
> **the glory of the LORD shall be thy rereward.**

One of the scriptures that the Lord used as a tool to help me to know what to do while using sackcloth is *Neh 9:1-3*. According to this scripture the assembly confessed their sins and the sins and iniquities of their ancestors, parents, grandparents, and so on. We must do the same for our ancestors and all those before us all the way back to Adam and Eve.

It says in the word that anything that is not of faith is sin and all unrighteousness is sin. We must ask the Lord to forgive them and us for everything and anything. I believe this will liberate all of us.

> *Now on the twenty-fourth day of this month*
> *the sons of Israel* **assembled with fasting,**

> *in sackcloth and with dirt upon them.*
> *The descendants of Israel separated themselves from all foreigners, and* **stood and confessed their sins and the iniquities of their fathers.** *While they stood in their place,* **they read from the book of the law of the LORD their God** *for a fourth of the day; and for another fourth* **they confessed and worshiped the LORD their God.**
> <u>Neh 9:1-3 NASB 1995</u>

In the New Testament it mentions that the dead will rise first and they will be incorruptible and we shall be changed with incorruption and immortality:

> *For the Lord himself shall descend from heaven with a shout, with the voice of the archangel, and with the trump of God: and* **the dead in Christ shall rise first:**
> <u>1 Thessalonians 4:16 KJV</u>

> *In a moment, in the twinkling of an eye, at the last trump: for the trumpet shall sound, and* **the dead shall be raised incorruptible, and we shall be changed.**
> *For this corruptible must put on incorruption, and this mortal must put on immortality So when this corruptible shall have put on incorruption, and this mortal shall have put on immortality, then shall be brought to pass the saying that is written, Death is swallowed up in victory.*

> *O death, where is thy sting?*
> *O grave, where is thy victory?*
> 1 Cor 15:52-55 KJV

It is our responsibility to make up for our ignorance and thoughtlessness toward the dead and those whom we have loved, even those who have hurt or abused us in any way. I know some sins such as abusive behavior, physical or mental may seem unforgiveable, or actions such as that of Hitler, but WE MUST FORGIVE! We must attempt to relieve ourselves of any bitterness, hatred, anger, resentments, and judgements that are making us ill. It is time to forgive the worst of sinners. And at least desire to love them!

Is there a measure of which sins are worse than others? I think not, they are all sins! To hate is like murder, to rebel like divination (witchcraft), when one lies, they lie to God and not to man, and God only knows what else or how else heaven compares or measures our sins. Many times, we think we are better than others, thinking our sins are lesser, Lord forgive us!

> *He who sins is of the devil,*
> *for the devil has sinned from the beginning.*
> *For this purpose the Son of God was manifested,*
> *that He might destroy the works of the devil.*
> 1 John 3:8 NKJV

Let us then pray that the Lord will loosen all evil held in our earthen vessels, and those sins that are unknown to us or may have been carried from generation to generation. Let us pray that He will undo the heavy burdens, and let the oppressed go free. Let us pray that He will give us the grace to break every yoke. Let us pray that He will unite us to Himself, that we may truly be set free and that the power of God may be in us, where no evil can touch or harm.

DRAW NEAR TO THE LORD...

It is time for us to draw near to Our Lord! Jesus came to convert us, transform us and unite us to Himself.

> *We know that no one who has been born of God sins; but He who was born of God keeps him, and the evil one does not touch him.*
> *1 John 5:18 NASB*

One who is born of God, does not sin, cannot sin, and the evil one cannot touch him. This is our goal, to be born of God. We must desire it!

> *[49] "I have come to cast fire upon the earth; and how I wish it were already kindled!*
> *[50] **But I have a baptism to undergo, and how distressed I am until it is accomplished!***
> *[51] Do you think that I came to provide peace on earth? No, I tell you, but rather division;*
> *Luke 12:49-51 NASB*

> [5]Jesus answered, "Very truly I tell you, no one can enter the kingdom of God unless they are born of water and the Spirit.
> [6]Flesh gives birth to flesh,
> **but the Spirit [b]gives birth to spirit.**

> ⁷You should not be surprised at my saying,
> 'You ᶜmust be born again.'
> ⁸The wind blows wherever it pleases.
> You hear its sound, but you cannot tell where it comes from or where it is going.
> **So it is with everyone born of the Spirit."**
> *John 3:5-8 NIV*

This baptism will be administered by the Lord Himself, "Spirit to Spirit" not by man. It is time to forgive everyone and ask the Lord to also forgive them. **It is time to also forgive the Lord for our trials and tribulations**, he asks for forgiveness every time we pray the Our Father.

The Lord is waiting for our contrition and mercy toward others. We must be merciful as Our Lord is merciful. There is a healing in this for each of us, for all of us as a unit, and for the deceased.

MY PRAYERS WILL BE ANSWERED

Years ago, the Lord led me to write three books. I never intended to write. In those years, when I was praying with people sometimes, I knew they were being helped. I also knew that the words that came out of my mouth were not mine. I began to write down the prayers immediately afterwards, otherwise I would forget what I said. And so, the first book was created: ***ONE**, One Love, One Hope, One God.*

However, I never promoted the books. After so many years of allowing the three books to be dormant, I got a call from two different publishers regarding the same book, in the same week.

With all my heart, I believe the Lord is presently moving the last of the three entitled:

THE GREAT DELIVERANCE *Stop a Grieving World*

The original book is being republished in 2023.

Why do I think my prayers will be answered? And which ones are they? On December 19th, 2005 I was somewhat asleep and saw a woman at a great distance like in a dream, she spoke to me in King James language. I repeated it three times, in King James language, however when I awoke, I could not say it verbatim. The content of the message is this:

> **"Your prayers are blessed and the Lord has heard them and He will answer"**

I was wondering which prayers the Lord would answer. I concluded that they would be the ones in the books. The prayers in the books are many, some biblically supported, some of them request perfect love, unconditional forgiveness, mercy, deliverance and more.

Of course, I do not know, what the Lord is going to do. However, in answer to my prayers, I believe the great deliverance is coming in my lifetime. Our Lord is faithful, and I believe He will do as the messenger told me. He will answer my prayers.

Could it be that the dead in Christ will rise first and we will be changed? Or could it be the rapture or the Baptism the Lord Himself wants to bestow upon us as mentioned in *Luke 12:49-51.* Will it be as it was for the apostles? Only He knows.

However, I believe this Baptism to be one that will fill us with grace upon grace, when we sin no more, and the evil one cannot touch us. This is when the excellency of the power of God is in us as mentioned in 2 Cor 4:7. I hope to be ready.

I pray that we will all be one and unified in Our Lord's Unconditional Love, Unconditional Mercy, Unconditional Forgiveness, and Unconditional Repentance **for all to be saved**.

UNCONDITIONAL MERCY!

THE GOOD NEWS is this: **that through our mercy, the Lord will be merciful even to the unbeliever.** This is synonymous with the story of Jonah, first the people repented then the Lord repented. Unconditional mercy!

> [26]*And so all Israel shall be saved: as it is written,*
> [28]*... they are enemies for your sakes: but*
> *..., they are beloved for the fathers' sake*
> [29]*For the gifts and calling of God are without repentance.*
> *For as ye in times past have not believed God,*
> *yet have now obtained mercy through their unbelief:*
> [31]***Even so have these also now not believed,***
> ***THAT THROUGH YOUR MERCY***
> ***THEY ALSO MAY OBTAIN MERCY.***
> [32]*For God hath concluded them all in unbelief,*
> ***that he might have mercy upon all.***
> Ro 11:26-32 KJV

> *"He who is without sin among you,*
> *let him be the first to throw a stone at her...*
> *⁹Now when they heard this,*
> *they began leaving, one by one,*
> *beginning with the older ones,*
> *and He was left alone, and the woman ...*
> *Jesus said to her, "Woman, where are they?*
> ***Did no one condemn you?"***
> *¹¹She said, "No one, [a]Lord."*
> *And Jesus said,*
> ***"I do not condemn you, either.***
> *Go. From now on do not sin any longer."*
> <u>John 8:7-11 NASB</u>

Please help me, help them! Help each other!
Love unconditionally! Be merciful to all!
We are all sinners!

I give to you my love in the Holy Family, may we all be part of it!

SACKCLOTH & ASHES

IN THE NEW TESTAMENT:

Sackcloth and Ashes are mentioned in the New Testament: <u>Luke 10:13, Mat 11:21 and Rev 11:3.</u> The following verse has a hidden message of great importance:

> *But He answered and said to them, "An evil and adulterous generation craves for a sign and yet no sign will be given to it but the sign of Jonah the prophet;* <u>Matthew 12:39</u>

WHAT IS THE SIGN OF JONAH?

The Sign of Jonah is the resulting salvation of the people and the beasts (animals) through true bitter repentance with the use of sackcloth and ashes.

THE SIGN OF JONAH

I was watching an animated Bible story about Jonah and was amazed at what I saw and heard. I will tell you the story as revealed to me: Jonah had a dream. The Lord wanted him to preach repentance in Niveth, a wicked city. Jonah did not like what he saw in his dream and did not want to obey the Lord. He decided to run away from the Lord, so he got on a boat going the opposite direction from Niveth. When the captain of the boat and his crew saw Jonah, they laughed at him, believing he was running away from his wife. The boat left dock, and began its journey, only to find itself in a great storm. The captain and the crew were frightened fearing their death. They apparently were men of God, obedient and of great faith, ready to offer their first fruits to Our Lord. The captain in fear of his life, told the crew to **Throw Everything Overboard as An Offering to The Lord** to appease his anger. The storm continued. The captain told the crew members to get Jonah who was below deck, so that he could pray to his God for the safety of the crew. When they brought Jonah out, they decided to cast lots to determine to whom the Lord was displaying his anger. They pointed at Jonah. Jonah told them to throw him overboard and that the storm would calm. The captain, a good man, did not want to do that. However, the storm continued and there was no other choice, they asked the Lord to forgive them and that they would do as Jonah had said. Jonah was then swallowed by a great fish in whose belly he remained for three days. Jonah repented and made a vow to the Lord, that if he would save him, he would preach repentance as the Lord had asked. The fish spit him out on land and Jonah did as he promised.

Jonah went to the city of Niveth and was preaching repentance. Three men that heard him went to the king and told the King that Jonah was preaching that all must repent or the Lord would destroy the whole city in a day. The king knowing that Jonah was a true prophet, tore off his clothes and put on sackcloth and sat in ashes. He then made a decree that the whole city People and Animals do the same, REPENT AND PUT ON **SACKCLOTH AND ASHES.**

After having preached Jonah went out of the city to high ground where he could view the city, waiting for God's wrath to destroy them. He waited and waited for a sign of destruction. In the heat of the sun, he became frustrated and angry that it had not yet happened.

The Lord then allowed a huge tree to grow in a day. Jonah was happy because the Lord provided shade for him. That night the Lord allowed worms to eat the tree. The next day Jonah was angry that the tree was gone and he was once again in the hot burning sun.

The Lord then spoke to Jonah and asked him why he was angry. He said you are angry that I have destroyed a tree that I created in a day and it is only one tree for which you did not toil. Yet you wait for me to destroy a city that has listened to your preaching and has repented.

I AM A MERCIFUL GOD; **MY PEOPLE HAVE REPENTED AND SO DO I REPENT.**

I LOVE MY PEOPLE, HUNDREDS OF THOUSANDS WHO HAVE LISTENED TO YOUR MESSAGE OF REPENTANCE ARE SAVED BECAUSE THEY HAVE REPENTED.

The Sign of Jonah is the resulting salvation of the people and the beasts (animals) through true bitter repentance with the use of sackcloth and ashes.

These are the items of significance in the story of Jonah.

1. We must be willing to give all - offer our first fruits to the Lord, even ourselves
2. Prayer, Trust, and Faith
3. Preaching Repentance and Repent
4. Use of Sackcloth and Ashes

5. Not just for People but Animals too
6. Stop wickedness! Desire to change your ways!
7. When the people repented, God Himself repented

(The measure you use is the measure you are measured with)
THEN PEOPLE REPENTED **THEN GOD REPENTED!**

WHAT IS SACKCLOTH AND ASHES?

Definitions

Sackcloth: *A coarse cloth of camel's hair, goat hair, hemp or flax. ie: Burlap*

Ashes: *The remains of something burned; ie: paper, blessed palm; charcoal*

Loins: *The region of the hips, groin, and lower abdomen; The reproductive organs.*

HOW TO USE SACKCLOTH & WHAT TO DO!

Initially I felt odd using Sackcloth. In 2004 I burned newspaper in an aluminum pan to make ashes. I then put them in a zip lock bag for later use. I obtained a stinky burlap cloth used by landscaping companies to gather their earthly remnants. I washed the burlap since it was treated. Not knowing how to use it, the Lord led me to *Isaiah 58:5*. In my backyard I chose an area big enough to lay the burlap. I spread ashes on the ground and put the burlap on top of the ashes. I laid face down on the burlap and my dog automatically sat next to me. I then began to pray, read scripture, and confess as the Lord had led me to understand in Neh 9:1. After completing this act of obedience, I went inside and read the Word again, the Lord fixed my eyes on, led my hands to *Psalm 30:11*. The Lord turned my mourning into dancing and loosed my sackcloth requirement.

Praise the Lord and repent with me, I believe that our act of faith will help all to be saved. After I did the above, I had a love for the sackcloth and used it as a quilt at night to sleep with, at which time I would also pray and continue in repentance asking the Lord to change me and to help me come to total obedience.

July 2022 the Lord enlightened me as mentioned in *What should my greatest and most Passionate Desire be?* and *Who are the 144000? Can we be part of that number?* in the book **THE GREAT DELIVERANCE – *Stop a Grieving World, Raptured by the Call to Heaven*** (Revised 2023). I attribute it to the fact that I was drawn to use sackcloth again. The Lord is teaching me, perhaps because I sleep in sackcloth. I am asking the Lord about its use; I still do not understand it. I am learning at a very slow pace; the Lord is gentle to teach. Perhaps the sackcloth provides a clearance for the Lord to teach us. It is not like I am sleeping in it and I know whatever He wants me to know. The knowledge comes in unexpected times, maybe driving home from work, anywhere, in little bits, in different ways. God is very creative! It took me months to learn how to use the sackcloth and ashes. I have a small brain compared to His. I am not special - He wants to teach you too!

> [10] *"For this is the Covenant that I will make with the house of Israel after those days, says the lord:*
> ***I WILL*** put m*y laws into their minds,*

> *And **I WILL** write them on their hearts.*
> *And **I WILL** be their God,*
> *and they shall be my people.*
> *¹¹"And **THEY SHALL NOT TEACH EVERYONE** his fellow citizen, and everyone his brother, saying, 'know the Lord,'*
> ***FOR ALL WILL KNOW ME,***
> ***From The Least To The Greatest Of Them**.*
> *¹²"For I Will be merciful to their iniquities,*
> ***AND I WILL REMEMBER THEIR SINS NO MORE."***
> <u>Heb 8:10-12 NASB95</u>

> *²⁶These things I have written to you concerning those who are trying to deceive you. ²⁷As for you, the anointing which you received from Him abides in you, **and you have no need for anyone to teach you;** but as His anointing teaches you about all things, and is true and is not a lie, and just as it has taught you, you abide in Him.*
> <u>1 John 2:26-27 NASB95</u>

The Lord is our teacher, our master, Our Rabbi, Our Father, Our Creator, Our all in all.

YOU MAY WEAR IT:
- Clothe yourself in sackcloth/wear sackcloth Tear off your clothes/remove them anxiously/change your Clothes;
- Cover your loins/body with sackcloth

- You may also put rope of hemp upon your head as a crown
- In Jonah the King wore sackcloth and sat in ashes.

YOU MAY LAY ON IT:
- fall on your face/lay in sackcloth;
- spread out sackcloth & ashes on a bed and lay on it

ASHES AND EARTH:
- put on you/roll/wallow in ashes,
- cast dust/dirt on your head
  _ put earth/ashes upon you; roll in dirt/ashes;
- sit in ashes
- fill a salt shaker with ashes and put on your food
  <u>Psalm 102:9; Isaiah 44:20</u>
  Eat ashes like bread, mingle weeping with drink

WHERE CAN I DO THIS:
- present yourself in Church in sackcloth and ashes and pray
- in home or outside; do not be ashamed to be humble to God who sees you and hears you
  _ **do not be deceived to remove the sackcloth from you/ it is for the Lord, that He may hear our prayer of repentance/the destroyer will come suddenly, put on sackcloth**

(The two witnesses in the book of Revelations are perfect examples; In *<u>Esther 4:4</u>* Mordechai refused to take off his sackcloth)

WHAT YOU MUST DO ONCE YOU HAVE IT ON OR ARE LAYING OR SITTING ON IT

- Cry mightily unto God, Wail/Mourn/weep/cry out loud bitterly, as loosing what or whom you love most and especially that the Lord will save everyone including those least lovable or the worst of sinners
  _ Beg the Lord desperately as He was desperate for our love allowing His son to die for us; surely even Our Father in Heaven cried out bitterly at the torment of His Beloved Son
  _ prostrate yourself before the Lord;
  _ Every one turn from our evil ways and from Violence. Desire to please the Lord; REPENT!
- PRAY; pray that their life and ours will be healed; salvation for the world
- FAST; Humble yourself before the Lord

For our beloved Dead

Scripture reference is *2 Samuel 21:10*: There was a famine for 3 yrs. David asked the Gibonites what could he do for them as atonement so that the Lord would restore their inheritance. They asked to hang seven sons of the man who was trying to kill them. King David granted that request.

Rizpah, who bore two of the sons of Saul which were hanged, spread sackcloth on top of rock, from the beginning of harvest until it rained. After King David found out what she did, he took the bones of King Saul and Jonathan and buried them. The Lord was moved by prayer and restored their inheritance.

NOW WHAT DO I DO???

Nehemiah 9 and *Daniel 9* inspired this response: Read Scripture, confess sins (see list) yours and your fathers, boldly and loudly while on or in sackcloth as taken from the Bible, also Worship the Lord.

According to *Nehemiah 9* they did the following:

1. Assembled with fasting in sackcloth with Dirt or ashes on them.
2. Confessed their sins and those of their fathers.
3. They read of the book of the law (Bible).
4. They worshipped the Lord.

> *Now on the twenty-fourth day of this month the sons of Israel* **assembled with fasting, in sackcloth and with dirt upon them.** *The descendants of Israel separated themselves from all foreigners, and* **stood and confessed their sins and the iniquities of their fathers.** *While they stood in their place,* **they read from the book of the law of the LORD their God** *for a fourth of the day; and for another fourth* **they confessed and worshiped the LORD their God.**
> *Neh 9:1-3 NASB95*

> *in the first year of his reign, I, Daniel, observed in the books the number of the years which was revealed as the word of the LORD to Jeremiah the prophet for the completion of the desolations of Jerusalem, namely, seventy years. So I gave my attention to the Lord God to* **seek Him by prayer**

and supplications, with fasting, sackcloth and ashes. Dan 9:2-3 NASB95

*Now while I was speaking and praying, and **confessing my sin and the sin of my people Israel**, and presenting my supplication before the LORD my God in behalf of the holy mountain of my God, Dan 9:20 KJV*

PRAY WITH YOUR OWN WORDS

Here Is A Start:

BREAK EVERY YOKE (inspired by *Isaiah 58*) Lord, please teach me to bow down in an acceptable way and to be pleasing to You. Help me to trust you and to acknowledge you in all my ways. Give to me wisdom, knowledge and understanding. Teach me to be obedient. Lead me to those whom you want me to help. Make me and Mold me to be the repairer of the breach, the restorer of paths to dwell in, as you desire, that the yoke of many will be broken. Teach me to draw out my soul to the hungry, and to satisfy the afflicted soul. Guide me continually and like a spring of water, let not my waters fail. Please allow my health to spring forth speedily. Teach me to keep the Sabbath holy as a delightful day unto the Lord, that you may feed me with the heritage of Jacob our father. All Glory, Honor and Power are Yours Most Beloved Heavenly Father in the Name of Jesus. Amen.

After prayer, confess your sins and those of your family and dead relatives, and all deceased, that perhaps the Lord will

be merciful to them. Do not point the finger, claim the sins as your own, but confess as "us" a unit.

SUGGESTED SCRIPTURES TO READ

For Man and Beast (Animals)
as noted in the Bible - (Animals included in Jonah):

SCRIPTURES:
Genesis 37:34; 2 Samuel 3:31;
2 Kings 6:30; 2 Kings 19:1-2; 1 Chronicles 21:16;
1 Kings 20:31-32; 1 Kings 21:21-27; Nehemiah 9:1;
Ester 4:1; Ester 4:3-4; Daniel 9:3; Jonah 3:6;
Jonah 3:8; Jeremiah 6:26; Jeremiah 25:34; Ezekiel 27:30;
Luke 10:13; Matthew 11:21; Revelation 11:3

Additional suggested (optional) scriptures to read:
Lamentations; Gospels; Daniel 3:26-44; Judith 9;
Matthew Ch 5 and 6; Matthew Ch 22:36-46; Exodus Ch 20;
Isaiah 58; Colossians 3:1-17; Daniel 3:52-90; Psalm 95-96

IN THE OLD TESTAMENT

> **_When I made sackcloth my clothing,_**
> **_I became a byword unto them._**
> _Ps 69:11 NASB95_

> **_I have sewed sackcloth upon my skin,_**
> **_and have laid my horn in the dust._**
> _Job 16:15ASV_

But as for me, when they were sick,
my clothing was sackcloth:
I afflicted my soul with fasting;
and my prayer returned into mine own bosom.
Ps 35:13 ASV

*³¹..."Look now, we have heard that the kings of the house of Israel are merciful kings. Please**, let us put sackcloth around our waists and ropes around our heads**, and go out to the king of Israel; perhaps he will spare your life."*
1 Ki 20:31 NKJV

O daughter of my people put on sackcloth
and roll in ashes, mourn as for an only son,
a lamentation most bitter.
For suddenly the destroyer will come upon us.
Jer 6:26 NASB95

ISAIAH 58 BE HEALED BREAK EVERY YOKE

⁵Is it such a fast that I have chosen?
a day for a man to afflict his soul?
is it to bow down his head as a bulrush,
*and **to spread sackcloth and ashes under him**?*
wilt thou call this a fast,
and an acceptable day to the LORD?

⁶Is not this the fast that I have chosen?
to loose the bands of wickedness,
to undo the heavy burdens,

*and to let the oppressed go free,
and that ye break every yoke?*

⁷*Is it not to* **deal thy bread to the hungry**, *and that thou* **bring the poor that are cast out to thy house?** *when thou seest* **the naked, that thou cover him**; *and that thou hide not thyself from thine own flesh?*

⁸**Then shall thy light break forth as the morning, and thine health shall spring forth speedily: and thy righteousness shall go before thee; the glory of the LORD shall be thy rereward.**

⁹*Then shalt thou call, and* **the LORD shall answer;** *thou shalt cry, and he shall say,* **Here I am. If thou take away from the midst of thee the yoke, the putting forth of the finger, and speaking vanity;**

¹⁰*And if thou draw out thy soul to the hungry, and satisfy the afflicted soul; then shall thy light rise in obscurity, and thy darkness be as the noon day:*

¹¹*And the LORD shall guide thee continually, and satisfy thy soul in drought, and make fat thy bones: and thou shalt be like a watered garden, and like a spring of water, whose waters fail not.*

¹²*And they that shall be of thee shall build the old waste places:* **thou shalt raise up the foundations of many generations; and thou shalt be called,**

The repairer of the breach, The restorer of paths to dwell in.

¹³If thou turn away thy foot from the sabbath, from doing thy pleasure on my holy day; and **call the sabbath a delight, the holy of the LORD, honourable; and shalt honour him,
not doing thine own ways,
nor finding thine own pleasure,
nor speaking thine own words:**

¹⁴Then shalt thou delight thyself in the LORD; and I will cause thee to ride upon the high places of the earth, and feed thee with the heritage of Jacob thy father: for the mouth of the LORD hath spoken it. Isaiah 58:5-14 KJV

SINS TO CONFESS WHILE USING SACKCLOTH & ASHES

(If you do not have sack cloth, ashes or dirt, confess anyway for yourself and for others throughout the world and even our own families with a contrite heart, mind and soul, and a bitter appeal to the Lord- I have no idea how the Lord would give measure to your actions without the sackcloth, but acting in faith is better than nothing). I have also confessed these in the confessional wearing my scapular made of wool: (We all have many of the same sins, add yours)

But first pray: **an act of faith**: Lord we believe that all sinners are blameless, for You are Commander, Master, Rabbi, Father,

Creator of all creation and as you command so it is done... We with all our hearts, mind and soul, love you and forgive you for allowing our trials, tribulations and hardships in our lives! Forgive our disobedience and rebellion against you. Heal Babylon!

Forgive us Lord for ....
- doubting your word and for our disbelief.
- leaning on human understanding.
- our ignorance and lack of desire to know you as you want us to
- for our wasted time ...
- all the times we do not believe, do not love, do not adore, and do not trust you, forgive our past sins also in this regard
- for the things we have done that we should not have done, and for the things we have failed to do
- the things we have said that we should not have said and for not saying the things we should have said
- our evil thoughts
- all our sins, especially those unknown to us.
- the harm and hurt we have caused others
- for causing others to sin resulting from our words or actions
- for exalting ourselves because of what we have made of ourselves or achieved
- for provoking or grieving others
- hurting members of our families, spouses, children, relatives and those near to us, including those who are deceased,
- breaking every commandment, ordinance, precept, and statutes of the Lord and not knowing what they are

- for the times we have killed even your smallest creation, or insulted those we love causing our relationships to die.
- For all the times I have broken the ten commandments of Our Lord, the commandments on the renewed tablets and the greatest commandments and for contributing to the sins of others who have broken them because of me
    o Using your name in vain
    o Having other gods before You
    o Making idols of any likeness of what is in heaven above or on the earth beneath or in the water under the earth
    o all the times our hands have created or touched works that are an abomination in your sight
    o For the idols our hands have created made of gold, silver, brass, stone, wood, molten or cast which can neither see, nor hear, nor walk (_Rev 9:20_)
    o For not acknowledging You in all that I say and do and, in my works,
    o For giving praise and worship to others who have been hidden to us as false gods or for giving you reason to be jealous,
    o every false god in our lives and on earth, whom we have served including those unknown to us.
    o Kneeling or bowing down to statues
    o Lifting my eyes to the idols of the house of Israel (_Ez 18:6_)
    o Not keeping the Sabbath as a day of rest, a holy day, a delight unto the Lord and for doing our own thing and speaking our own words on the Sabbath
    o the times I have worked, carried a load, bought, or sold and did not rest. Please forgive also those who

worked with me, helped me or made me to work. Forgive the intent of my heart and the errors I have incurred because of my ignorance and otherwise, done with intent.

- For all the times I have dishonored my parents on earth
- For all the times I have dishonored Our Blessed Mother Mary, Jesus, Our Heavenly Father, and all that He has created
- stirring the wrath of God because of our disobedience
- the sins of hatred, murder, anger, wrath, malice, blasphemy, filthy communication out of our mouth, drunkenness, jealousies, abusiveness, laziness, judgments, prejudices and condemnation, pride and for not repenting.
- our selfishness, greed, rebellion, and self-centeredness
- fornication, adultery, uncleanness, inordinate affection, evil concupiscence, and covetousness, which is idolatry
- stealing and manipulating others for our own benefit, and for making them to suffer the consequences
- bearing false witness, lying, gossiping, and putting stumbling blocks in the path of my brethren
- idle words and careless speech spoken in the past, present and in the future
- vain glory, pride of life and lust of the flesh and lust of the eyes
- For all the times I have served money in a book fold wallet and making others to desire more money (ie waitresses), for thinking we need it to survive

- For yearning to possess (coveting) my neighbor's house, wife, servants, animals, possessions, or anything that belongs to him
- For not being content with my pay, and for not trusting in divine providence
- For making covenants with the inhabitants of the land and allowing them to become a snare
- For not understanding and not knowing how to keep the Feast of Unleavened Bread from generation to generation
- For not offering the first offspring from every womb, and the first male son born to the Lord
- For not celebrating three times a year, the Feast of Weeks and Feast of Ingathering out of ignorance, quite frankly Lord, I don't know how, you have kept me in the dark
- FORGIVE MY ANGER LORD- for relying on men to pass down your laws that you wanted fulfilled from generation to generation, we are weak, you are strong. Only you could have faithfully guided us to do as You have instructed. Forgive us, we forgive you Surely, we are deserving of the punishment for what we have done and the anguish we have lived in this world, We ask that you demonstrate your mercy Lord and deliver us from this evil! Banish all that is not pleasing to you! Make of us a new creation and guide us in all things, teach us your ways. Only You can set things right.
- For all the times the blood of your sacrifice has been offered with leavened bread
- For the leftovers from the Feast of the Passover which were left until morning

- o For boiling a young goat in its mother's milk
- For being proud of our accomplishments,
- For loving everything we might have acquired in this world and those things unknown to us
- For the times we have loved our spouse, children, home, things, groups, and not acknowledged or loved you first
- The times I have caused oppression to someone and have not paid my debt
- for not forgiving debt after a seven year period
- not denying ourselves as we should,
- the times I have babbled in prayer heartlessly
- the times I have not prayed pleasing to you with all heart, mind and soul
- only praying out of need or distress.
- our inequities and the inequities of our fathers and relatives, especially of those deceased that might still be suffering for their sins whom you have judged.
- participating in thoughts that have altered your word from Bible to Bible, from generation to generation; forgive those that have altered it for others to see and hear.
- all the times we have spoken false doctrine and for teaching others that false doctrine.
- participating in the sins of all religious preachers, teachers, leaders, helpers, listeners, forgive them Lord their sins
- the veil that has kept us from you,
- Concealing your truth from others
- all the times we destroy the work of Your hands
  - by poisoning our earth, plants and flowers
  - killing creatures great and small
  - contaminating the waters

- attempting to take creation into our own hands by cloning, reproductive services, birth control, abortions, subrogation of mothers, euthanasia, science
* all the sins I have committed for not having lived in your faith, for you said that all that is not faith is sin
* for our unrighteousness which is sin
* all the times we disagree with your truth
* also forgive anyone who comes against the truth written in this book, and forgive me for writing anything in this book that is not true, may only truth excel
* not mortifying our members which are upon the earth;
* the sins of my members, my eyes, my ears, my mouth, my tongue, my limbs, my body, and my whole being for we are one
* the times I have been defiled or allowed my husband to approach me during my menstrual period (*Ez 18:6*)
* for my unchastity against my Lord
* receiving Holy Communion unworthily
* eating and drinking judgment
* Judging my food and drink and all creatures and creation of the earth and all judgements against visible and invisible as created by my Lord
* not judging the body rightly
* not serving others properly
* not demonstrating the fruits of the spirit as I should
* the sins of the spirit of gluttony and for my depraved passions.
* wanting things of the earth and for thinking that I need them
* for my distracted devotion pulling me away from You Lord

- causing others to sin because of my words, actions or deeds
- sinning against others, please forgive those who have sinned against me
- addictions and passions we have attached ourselves to, being snared by them
- the addictions tormenting my children and those addictions they suffer resulting from my sins
- all things that offend you and others
- for not resting as I should
- for all the times I have resisted loving my enemies
- for not having the greatest love
- for partiality and favoritism
- for breaking promises, I could not keep or did not intend to keep
- sinning against You and against others and against myself.
- For obeying man rather than God
- cutting our body for the dead
- making tattoo marks on ourselves

'You shall not make any cuts in your body for the dead nor make any tattoo marks on yourselves: I am the LORD. Le 19:28

- not clothing myself in the armor of God, in the armor of righteousness and justice (*2Cor 6:7*)
- not having desired to have a mind of Christ (*1Cor 2:16*)
- not seeking you sooner
- not blessing our enemies as we should,
- not feeding the hungry,
- not giving shelter to the poor,

- not giving freely what the Lord has given to me
- not clothing the naked
- not being the repairer of the breach, the restorer of the path to dwell in.

ADDITONAL SINS – WOES IN THE BOOK OF MATTHEW

But first: **an act of faith**: Lord we believe that all sinners, priests, scribes, pharisees, blind guides, and hypocrites are blameless, for You are Commander, Master, Rabbi, Father, Creator of all creation and as you command so it is done… We with all our hearts, mind and soul, love you and forgive you for allowing our trials, tribulations and hardships in our lives!

We desire to repent of the sins mentioned in the Woes in the book of Matthew, please also forgive those who have died and are suffering.

My thought is that we should confess these sins for ourselves as well, we do not know if any of our ancestors were scribes, priests, pharisees, blind guides and hypocrites. Let us cover every basis. Woe to you, scribes (maybe writers who corrupt the thoughts of men; maybe it is all writers, people who translate, transcribe, or are associated with changes to the Bible) and Pharisees (per dictionary they are those who follow the law and think of themselves of highest sanctity), blind guides and hypocrites

Forgive us Lord …
- For telling people to do works and for not doing it myself

- For binding heavy burdens, hard to bear and laying them on men's shoulders but not even trying to move them with one of my fingers
- For doing works only to be seen by men
- For loving the best places at feasts, the best seats in gatherings
- For being called Rabbi, Father, Teacher, Leader for there is only one and that is Christ
- For traveling land and sea to convert persons from one religion to another (proselyte) and making him twice as much as a son of hell as myself
- For shutting up the kingdom of heaven against men and not allowing them to enter in
- For devouring widow's houses
- For pretending to make long prayers
- For swearing by the gold of the temple or the gifts on the altar, that is, telling people to give so that the Lord will bless them
- For anytime I have ever sworn and should not have
- For neglecting weightier matters of the law: justice and mercy and faith
- For being a blind guide
- For cleansing the outside of the cup and dish, when inside they are full of extortion and self-indulgence
- For appearing beautiful outwardly but inside am full of dead men's bones and all uncleanness
- For appearing to be outwardly righteous to men but inside full of hypocrisy and lawlessness
- For building the tombs of the prophets and adorning the monuments of the righteous and saying "if we had lived in the days of our fathers, we would not have been partakers with them in the blood of the prophets"

- For the measure of my fathers' guilt, Serpents, brood of vipers that we have been
- For all the times we have killed the prophets and stoned those who are sent to Jerusalem
- For obeying men rather than God
- Woe to the rich, for all the times I have accepted riches and not distributed them to the poor
- Woe to the well fed, for indulging in feasts when others have much less or not sharing with the less fortunate
- For the times I have bought or sold on the sabbath
- For carrying a load or doing anything I should not have done on the sabbath
- For making others to sin on the Sabbath
- For indulging in my own pleasures on the Sabbath
- For doing my own thing, going my own way, speaking my own words on the Sabbath
- For enjoying this worldly life to the fullest being distracted from my devotion to the Lord
- For receiving praise from men
- For lending expecting in return
- For being blind and leading the blind
- For profaning the sabbath
- For allowing sales of religious articles in the churches, putting up stores in the church and having people work them on the Sabbath
- For not acknowledging you in my every thought, word or deed
- Forgive us Lord for partaking in the division of the churches,
- forgive us Lord for partaking in the division of the things we believe about You and Heaven and the saints

- forgive us Lord for the division of the belief in Blessed Mother Mary Most Holy
- Forgive us Lord for we and our ancestors have surely been of a wicked, evil and adulterous generation
- Forgive us Lord for seeking signs and wonders
- Forgive us Lord for not trusting in You as we should. Please give us the grace to Trust you unconditionally and to love you as you love us.

Thank You Lord for your great mercy and love. Blessed and Exalted are you Lord God of Glory, lover of my soul. You, Lord, are the Almighty, All Powerful, Creator of All, Lover of All. You speak and it is done.

All creatures obey you, the winds, the waters and even us in our disobedience.

You have allowed it for we are in training to be like You as you have said in Your Word. So, Lord, Job said you wound but you heal as well.

Heal us Oh Lord. Please allow our souls to magnify you and our spirit to rejoice in you. Make your joy complete, by making us of the same mind, maintaining the same love, united in spirit, intent on one purpose as mentioned in *Philippians 2:2. NASB*.

> All Glory Praise and Honor is Yours alone!
> Beloved King of Glory!
> Commander in Chief!
> God of All Creation!

WHY DID MARY PRESENT THE SCAPULAR AS A SIGN OF SALVATION?

The Sign of Jonah is the sign of salvation. It is the resulting salvation of the people and the beasts (animals) through true bitter repentance with the use of sackcloth and ashes.

> *See to it that you do not refuse Him who is speaking. For if those did not escape when they refused him who warned them on earth, much less will we escape who turn away from Him who warns from heaven.*
> Heb 12:25 NASB95

Mary presents a scapular to the world in more than one appearance. She said that anyone who dies wearing it will not suffer eternal fire. It is said to be "the sign of salvation."

I tell you now that this agrees with the "sign of Jonah". It is the sign of salvation with repentance and love. It is sack cloth and must be worn in cloth made of wool (or animal hair like camel as John the Baptist wore) as presented by Mary, Mother of God, most Blessed. I am not sure if the scapular satisfies Our Lord completely, but in the right state of grace, I know the Lord keeps His promises. Sister Faustina was asked by Our Lord to put on a shirt of hair clothe, her superior denied her. How sad! Should we all wear sackcloth?

The Lord will know his sheep by the wool that they wear! Repent and live a Christian life in love and mercy and wear it to please the Lord. Honor Our Lord and Our Blessed Mother by wearing this garment (100% wool scapular) so that you may not suffer eternal fire.

The Lord says if you love me, obey my Commands. You must strive to be in obedience to His Commandments. Desire to please the Lord and Our Blessed Mother, Mary, Mother of God!

The following was taken from this website:
http://www.truecatholic.org/scapular.htm
The Brown Scapular of Our Lady of Mt. Carmel

*A magnificent assurance of salvation is Our Lady's Brown Scapular. One of the great mysteries of our time is that the great majority of Catholics either ignore or have forgotten the Blessed Virgin Mary's promise that "**whoever dies wearing this (Scapular) shall not suffer eternal fire.**" She further says: "Wear it devoutly and perseveringly. It is my garment. To be clothed in it means you are continually thinking of me, and I in turn, am always thinking of you and helping you to secure eternal life."*

*Many Catholics may not know that it is the wish of our Holy Father, the Pope, that the Scapular **Medal should not be worn in place of the Cloth Scapular** without sufficient reason. Mary cannot be pleased with anyone who substitutes the medal out of vanity, or fear to make open profession of religion. Such persons run the risk of not receiving the Promise. The medal has never been noted for any of the miraculous preservations attributed to the Brown Cloth Scapular.*

During the Scapular Anniversary celebration in Rome, Pope Pius XII told a very large audience to wear the brown Scapular as a sign of consecration to the Immaculate Heart of Mary. Our Lady asked for this consecration in the last apparition at Fatima, when She appeared as Our Lady of Mount Carmel, holding the Brown Scapular out to the whole world. It was her last loving appeal to souls to wear her Scapular as a sign of Consecration to her Immaculate Heart.

Blessed Claude de la Colombiere, the renowned Jesuit and spiritual director of St. Margaret Mary, gives a point which is enlightening. He said: "Because all the forms of our love for the Blessed Virgin, all its various modes of expression cannot be equally pleasing to Her, and therefore do not assist us in the same degree to Heaven, I say without a moment's hesitation the BROWN SCAPULAR is the most favored of all!" He also adds: "No devotion has been confirmed by more numerous authentic miracles than the Brown Scapular."

Why should we wear it?

The scapular should be worn to honor Our Blessed Mother who has asked us to wear it. It is a devotion to Her. She promises that she will not let us fall into eternal fire by wearing the scapular. Wearing it all the time is a safeguard. It is a sign of salvation when worn made of wool. It is a form of trusting God and believing in His Mother hoping to obtain graces necessary to obtain the promises of God and reaching Heaven.

Brown **100% wool scapular** buy at Rose Scapular Company – shop around for better deals. Just make sure it is 100% wool.

TODAYS MESSAGE IS THIS

Repent In Sackcloth and Ashes!
Love unconditionally
and The Churches Must Unite!

Jesus came to convert, transform, and teach everyone. All Christ Believers must unite in unconditional love, so that the Lord can do Greater things! Presently, **the kingdom of God is divided.** A divided kingdom cannot stand as mentioned in Mark 3:24. So, let us finish this! Let us stand together! Enter the Lion's Den.

Love unconditionally!

The Lord has promised victory in the church of the apostle Peter: the Roman Catholic Church.

> *And I say also unto thee, That thou art Peter, and upon this rock I will build my church;* ***And The Gates Of Hell Shall Not Prevail Against It.*** *Mat 16:18 KJV*

This is the Lord's plea:

> [10]*Now* ***I BESEECH YOU, BRETHREN****, by the name of our Lord Jesus Christ, that ye all speak the same thing, and* ***THAT THERE BE NO DIVISIONS AMONG YOU****; but that ye be perfectly joined together in the same mind and in the same judgment.*
> *1 Corinthians 1:10 KJV*

Who will listen to the lifesaving commands of Our Lord? *Smear Your Door with The Blood of The Lamb! Do Not Look Back or You Will Turn into Stone! Build An Ark!* These lifesaving commands were given by Our Father in Heaven, No Bible, nothing written, except in the heart of the believer, trusting the messenger of God.

> *By this we know love,*
> *because He laid down His life for us.*
> ***And we also ought to lay down***
> ***our lives for the brethren***
> <u>*1 John 3:16 NKJV*</u>

<u>Neh 9 NASB95</u>:
> [5]*"Arise, bless the LORD your God forever and ever!*
> *O may Your glorious name be blessed*
> *And exalted above all blessing and praise!*
>
> [6]*"You alone are the LORD. You have made the heavens,*
> *The heaven of heavens with all their host,*
> *The earth and all that is on it,*
> *The seas and all that is in them.*
> *You give life to all of them*
> *and the heavenly host bows down before You.*
> [7]*"You are the LORD God, …*
>
> [17]*"… But You are a God of forgiveness,*
> *Gracious and compassionate,*
> *Slow to anger and abounding in lovingkindness;*
> *And You did not forsake them.*

³² "Now therefore, our God, the great, the mighty, and the awesome God, who keeps covenant and lovingkindness,
Do not let all the hardship seem insignificant before You, Which has come upon us,
...and on all Your people, From the days of the kings of Assyria to this day.

Grant us peace, harmony and relieve our hardships, heal our infirmities, remove every heavy burden, heal the oppressed, break every yoke, and deliver us from evil. Fill us with your Perfect Love. Make Your Joy complete by making us of the same mind, having the same love, unite us in the same spirit, intent on one purpose. Transform us to be love, and to love unconditionally. Redeem us Oh Lord. Thank you, Lord for your Great Compassion and Omnipotent Mercy! Perfect, transform and unite us to Yourself in Your perfect Love, in Jesus, in Mary and in all the holy ones who have reached perfection. Amen

BELIEVE!

In *Mat 21:32* the Lord says **that because you have not repented you do not believe**. This is the time to Repent.

> *For John came unto you in the way of righteousness, and ye believed him not: but the publicans and the harlots believed him: and ye, when ye had seen it,* ***repented not afterward, that ye might believe him.*** *Mat 21:32 KJV*

www.LovesTrueDesire.com

The End

LORD HEAR OUR PRAYER

Lord Hear our prayer, let the words of our mouth and the meditation of our hearts be acceptable to You every moment of our being in time and eternity.

Give to us a sincere desire to pray so that we may have a fervent soul of the righteous, so that our prayers may be pleasing to You. Teach us to pray with our whole heart mind and soul. Forgive us for leaning on human understanding and believing what man has taught falsely. Be Our Teacher, Our Leader, Our Guide, Our Rabbi, Our Father, Our All in All.

Make us to be heard by You – and as a Father to His children—answer us.

Forgive us Lord for not denying ourselves as we should, teach us how Lord, so that we may be pleasing to you.

Forgive us our inequities and the inequities of our fathers and relatives, especially of those deceased that might still be suffering for their sins whom you have judged. Bring them Lord to your everlasting Light that they may enter into eternal rest in your loving light and dwelling place which you have prepared for us. Make us Lord to repent pleasing to you.

Lord, we beseech you to **grant to us the grace of increased power of our prayers** that as one day is as a thousand days so then is one of our prayers **multiplied in your unfathomable love for the benefit of our brethren and those most in need of prayer.**

As you granted to Elisha a double portion of Elijah's spirit, so then, we ask the same for the benefit of our brethren. Lord, we also ask that you allow the whole church, all angels and saints to intercede for us in union with Mother Mary Most Holy. Please Lord, deliver us from evil. Thank you, Father for hearing our prayers in the Name of Jesus.

REFERENCES

PUBLIC DOMAIN BIBLES QUOTED:

ASV - Scriptural verses were used in this work from the ASV.

From Wikipedia: **The American Standard Version** (ASV) is rooted in the work that was done with the Revised Version (RV) (a late 19th-century British revision of the King James Version of 1611). In 1870, an invitation was extended to American religious leaders for scholars to work on the RV project. A year later, Protestant theologian Philip Schaff chose 30 scholars representing the denominations of Baptist, Congregationalist, Dutch Reformed, Friends, Methodist, Episcopal, Presbyterian, Protestant Episcopal, and Unitarian. These scholars began work in 1872.

The RV New Testament was released In 1881; the Old Testament was published in 1885. **The ASV was published in 1901** by Thomas Nelson & Sons. In 1928, the International Council of Religious Education (the body that later merged with the Federal Council of Churches to form the National Council of Churches) acquired the copyright from Nelson and renewed it the following year.

The divine name of the Almighty (the Tetragrammaton) is consistently rendered Jehovah in the ASV Old Testament, rather than LORD as it appears in the King James Bible.

The **ASV** was the basis of four revisions. They were the Revised Standard Version, 1971, the Amplified Bible, 1965, the New American Standard Bible, 1995, and the Recovery Version,

1999. **A fifth revision, known as the World English Bible, was published in 2000 and was placed in the public domain.** The ASV was also the basis for Kenneth N. Taylor's Bible paraphrase, The Living Bible, 1971.

This Bible is in the public domain in the United States. We are making it available in the same format in which we acquired it as a public service.

KJV - Scriptural verses were used in this work from the KJV. *Scripture quotations from The Authorized (King James) Version. Rights in the Authorized Version in the United Kingdom are vested in the Crown. Reproduced by permission of the Crown's patentee, Cambridge University Press.*

In 1604, King James I of England authorized that a new translation of the Bible into English be started. It was finished in 1611, just 85 years after the first translation of the New Testament into English appeared (Tyndale, 1526). The Authorized Version, or **King James Version**, quickly became the standard for English-speaking Protestants. Its flowing language and prose rhythm has had a profound influence on the literature of the past 400 years. The King James Version present on the Bible Gateway matches the 1987 printing. **The KJV is public domain** in the United States.

OTHER BIBLES QUOTED

NKJV – Biblehub Scriptural verses were used in this work from The Holy Bible, New King James Version, Copyright © 1982 Thomas Nelson. Used by permission. All rights reserved.

NASB – Scriptural verses were used in this work from NASB New American Standard Bible Sackcloth & Ashes | 49 Copyright © 1960, 1971, 1977, 1995, 2020 by The Lockman Foundation, La Habra, Calif. Used by permission. All rights reserved.
http://www.lockman.org

NASB 1995 - Scriptural verses were used in this work from NASB 1995 Copyright © 1960, 1962, 1963, 1968, 1971, 1972, 1973, 1975, 1977, 1995 by The Lockman Foundation, La Habra, Calif. Used by permission. All rights reserved.
http://www.lockman.org

WEBSITES USED AS REFERENCE

http://www.truecatholic.org/scapular.htm

www.ingramcontent.com/pod-product-compliance
Lightning Source LLC
LaVergne TN
LVHW092059060526
838201LV00047B/1477